Thank you to the generous team who gave their time and talents to make this book possible:

Author
Worku L. Mulat

Editor
Beth Abate Bacon

Illustrator
Daniel Getahun

Creative Directors
Caroline Kurtz, Jane Kurtz,
and Kenny Rasmussen

Translators
Alem Eshetu Beyene
Woubeshet Ayenew

Designer
Beth Crow

Ready Set Go Books, an Open Hearts Big Dreams Project

ISBN: 979-8671737271
Library of Congress Control Number: 2020922724

Republished: 11/29/20

Thirteen Months of Sunshine

አሥራ ሦስቱ ፀሐያማ ወራት

English and Amharic

Ethiopia is the only nation in East Africa with its own calendar. The calendar is seven to eight years behind the one used by most of the world.

በምሥራቅ አፍሪካ ውስጥ የራሷ ቀን መቁጠሪያ ያላት አገር ኢትዮጵያ ብቻ ናት። መቁጠሪያው ከብዙው ዓለም ከሰባት እስከ ስምንት ዓመት በሚሆን ወደኋላ የዘገየ ነው።

When most countries celebrated the year 2020, it was the year 2012 in Ethiopia.

አብዛኛዎቹ የዓለም አገሮች የ2020 አዲስ ዓመታቸውን ሲያከብሩ ኢትዮጵያ ውስጥ ገና 2012 ነበር።

The Ethiopian calendar has 13 months. Twelve of these months have 30 days: Meskerem, Tekemt, Hedar, Tahsas, Ter, Yekatit, Megabit, Miyazya, Genbot, Senay, Hamley, Nehassey.

የኢትዮጵያ ቀን መቁጠሪያ አሥራ ሦስት ወራት አሉት። ከነዚህም ውስጥ አሥራ ሁለቱ ወራት 30 ቀኖች አሏቸው። እነሱም መስከረም፣ ጥቅምት፣ ህዳር፣ ታህሣሥ፣ ጥር፣ የካቲት፣ መጋቢት፣ ሚያዝያ፣ ግንቦት፣ ሰኔ፣ ሐምሌ እና ነሐሴ ናቸው።

Daniel Getahun

The last month, Pagumey, has just five or six days. That is why Ethiopia is called a nation with 13 months of sunshine.

የመጨረሻዋ ወር ጳጉሜ ትባላለች፤ አምስት ወይም ስድስት ቀኖች አሏት። በዚህም ምክንያት ነው ኢትዮጵያ የአሥራ ሦስቱ ፀሐያማ ወራት አገር የምትባለው።

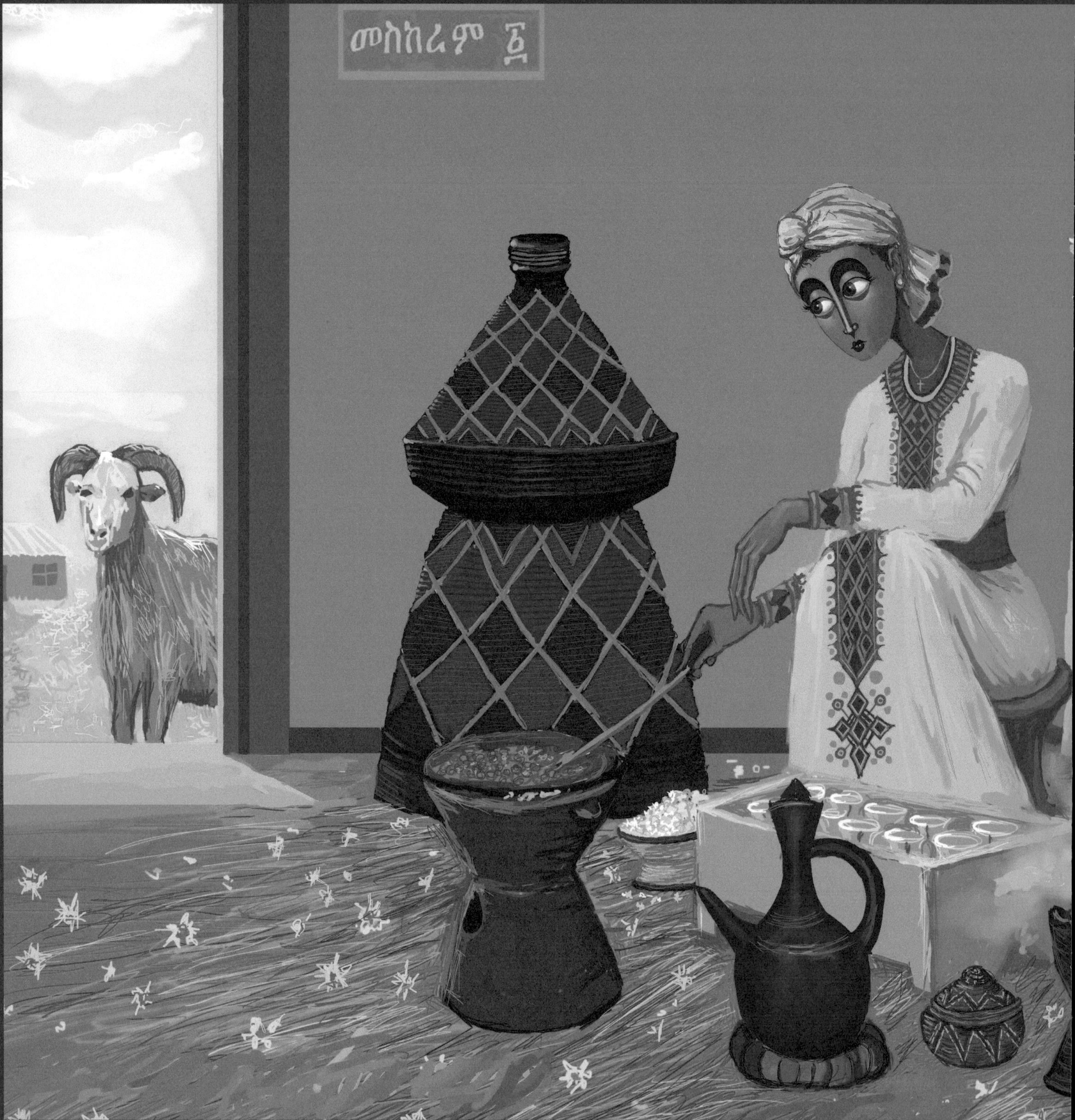
መስከረም ፩

The new year starts on the first day of the month called Meskerem. In many countries, that is the middle of the ninth month on the calendar.

የአዲስ ዓመት መስከረም በሚባለው ወር የመጀመሪያ ቀን ላይ ይውላል። ይኸም በብዙ አገሮች ቀን መቁጠሪያ መሰረት የዘጠነኛዉ ወር አጋማሽ ላይ የሚያርፍ ቀን ነው።

In most countries a day starts just after midnight. In Ethiopia, a day starts at dawn. The New Year starts at dawn on the first day of the year.

በአብዛኞቹ አገሮች አንድ ቀን የሚጀመምረው ልክ ከእኩለ ሌሊት በኋላ ነው። የኢትዮጵያ ቀኖች የሚጀምሩት ግን ጠዋት ሲነጋ ነው። ስለዚህም ኢትዮጵያ ውስጥ አዲሱ ዓመት የሚጀምረው የአመቱ የመጀመሪያው ቀን ሲነጋ ነው።

In Meskerem, the season changes. The countryside appears at its best. The rain stops pouring. Fields are covered with yellow, red and pink flowers.

መስከረም የወቅት መለወጫ ወር ነው። ገጠሩ በጣም ያምራል። ዝናብ ያቆማል። መስኮች በቢጫ፣ ቀይና ሐምራዊ አበቦች ይሸፈናሉ።

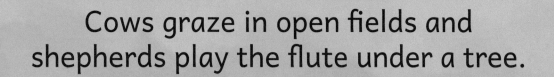

Cows graze in open fields and
shepherds play the flute under a tree.

ከብቶች በለምለም መስክ ላይ ሣር
ይግጣሉ፤ እረኞች ደግሞ በዛፍ ጥላ ስር
ቁጭ ብለው ዋሽንት ይነፋሉ።

Children go from house to house
and sing the New Year's song.

ልጆች ከቤት ወደ ቤት በመሄድ
የእንቁጣጣሽ ዘፈን እየዘፈኑ
በአሉን ያደምቃሉ።

People buy
chickens. They
cook a feast
to celebrate the
new year.

ሰዎች ዶሮ ይገዛሉ።
የድግስ ምግብ ሰርተው
አዲሱን አመት
ያከብራሉ።

The Ministry of Education hires new teachers. Parents buy textbooks, pencils and notebooks. Children are ready to return to school.

የትምህርት ሚንስትር አዳዲስ መምህራንን ይቀጥራል። ወላጆች መጽሐፍትን፣ እርሳስና ደብተሮችን ይገዛሉ። ልጆች ወደ ትምህርት ቤት ለመመለስ ይዘጋጃሉ።

The rainy season is over in Meskerem. A carpet of yellow daisies signals the beginning of the thirteen months of sunshine.

ክረምቱ መስከረም ሲጠባ ያበቃል።
የአደይ አበባ ምንጣፍም የአሥራ ሦስት
ወር ፀጋ መጀመሩን ያበሥራል።

About The Story

More than fifty years ago, Habte Selassie Tafesse—widely credited with starting the industry of tourism in Ethiopia—dreamed up the slogan, "Thirteen months of sunshine." He was looking for ways to intrigue potential visitors and highlight what makes Ethiopia distinctivewhen the catchy phrase came to him, based on the distinctive Ethiopian calendar. Since then, tourism has had some extremely successful years. In 2015, for example, the European Council on Tourism and Tradevoted Ethiopia as the world's best destination for tourists, highlighting its nine UNESCO World Heritage Sites, dramatic geography, and lovely sunshine.

About The Author

 Worku L. Mulat joined the Ready Set Go Books team early in 2019, first as a translator and now as an author. He holds a PhD from University College Cork in Ireland, an MSc from Gent University, Belgium, and a BSc from Asmara University, Eritrea. Dr. Worku has published extensively professional articles on high impact journals such as Malaria Journal, Environmental Monitoring and Assessment, Ecological Indicators, Bioresource Technology, and PLOS ONE. He also co-authored three books with a main theme of Environmental conservation. Currently he is working for Open Hearts Big Dreams Fund as Innovation Center Lead in Model projects being implemented in Ethiopia. He is also a research associate at Tree Foundation which strives to save Ethiopian Orthodox church forests.

About The Illustrator

 Daniel Getahun lives in Toronto, Canada. He received a diploma in graphic art from Addis Ababa School of Fine Arts and Design in 1980. He now focuses on oil painting and digital painting, which can be seen on his Facebook page. He can also be contacted by email: danielgetahun1@hotmail.com

About The Editor

Beth Abate Bacon is an author of books for young people. She earned an MFA in writing for children from Vermont College of Fine Arts. She also has a degree in communications from NYU and a degree in literature from Harvard. She previously worked with Apple on communications and marketing, as well as a teacher at the elementary and high school levels. Beth loves to travel and share stories about our world's varied cultures, traditions, and perspectives.

About Open Hearts Big Dreams

Open Hearts Big Dreams Fund (OHBD) was founded by Ellenore Angelidis, inspired by her Ethiopian born daughter, Leyla Marie Fasika; both are key volunteers. OHBD is a United State 501(c)(3) not-for-profit organization that believes the chance to dream big dreams should not depend on where in the world you are born. Our mission is "Inspiring and empowering youth (K-14) to reimagine their futures by providing literacy, STEAM, and leadership opportunities."

OHBD harnesses the power of collaboration. We are made up of a small number of part-time paid staff and a large number of highly motivated volunteers with advanced skills, including artistic, editorial, translation, and high-tech expertise in Ethiopia, the Diaspora and globally. Our culture of innovation means we act fast on new ideas. Since 2017, we've produced more than 700 bilingual, culturally appropriate early reader titles and a number of STEM and Model programs to increase literacy, inclusion, and leadership.

In Ethiopia, for Ethiopia; OHBD is based in the U.S. but we are committed to working with local content creators and to producing quality books in Ethiopia. Local opportunities and production builds local knowledge and capacity.

About OHBD Ready Set Go Books

Reading has the power to change lives, but many children and adults in Ethiopia cannot read. One reason is that Ethiopia doesn't have enough books in local languages to give people a chance to practice reading. Ready Set Go books wants to close that gap and open a world of ideas and possibilities for kids and their communities.

When you buy an OHBD-RSG book, you provide critical funding to create and distribute more books.

Learn more at: http://openheartsbigdreams.org/book-project/ or find all our books at: https://ohbd-rsgbooks.com

OHBD Proudly Prints in Ethiopia

OHBD developed our own local printing capacity and have a number of our books available to pick up in Addis. They are available for bulk purchase and we regularly donate to schools, libraries and local organizations serving kids. Please contact us at ellenore@openheartsbigdreams.org if interested in samples or ordering.

So far, we have printed and distributed (with collaborating organizations) hundreds of thousands of copies of our books in numerous languages in country.

Our goal is to get these books to all elementary students across Ethiopia.

About the Language

Amharic is a Semetic language -- in fact, the world's second-most widely spoken Semetic language, after Arabic. Starting in the 12th century, it became the Ethiopian language that was used in official transactions and schools and became widely spoken all over Ethiopia. It's written with its own characters, over 260 of them. Eritrea and Ethiopia share this alphabet, and they are the only countries in Africa to develop a writing system centuries ago that is still in use today!

About the Translation

Alem Eshetu Beyene taught translation at Addis Ababa University for three years and translated six books during that time. He also has taught Amharic and written a book called Amharic for Foreign Beginners. In addition, he has published a number of books for children that can be found in bookshops in Addis Ababa (and two on Amazon.com) and in schools where he donates copies for families that cannot afford to buy them.

Dr. Woubeshet Ayenew's role at Ready Set Go Books combines his passions for parenting and language. He is a cardiologist by training but parenting is his most demanding and wonderfully rewarding job. Once his children started to read and write in Amharic, he went out searching for child-friendly bilingual books. He eventually linked up with the creative team from Ready Set Go Books.

Though a resident of the US for over 30 years, he maintains a healthy grasp of his native language and culture; his shelves are filled with Amharic novels and other writings that he picks up during his regular medical mission trips to Ethiopia, and he assumes many roles in his Ethiopian community in Minnesota. He views every story in the Ready Set Go Books collection from the side of his Ethiopian-American children as well as from the perspective of the young readers of his native land. He knows the job is done when there is something wondrous for everyone in every story.

OPENHEARTS BIGDREAMS

Ready Set Go Books

Over 100+ unique OHBD-RSG books available in neary 20 languages!

 To view all available titles, go to https://ohbd-rsgbooks.com/shop or scan QR code

Open Heart Big Dreams is pleased to offer discounts for bulk orders, educators and organizations.

Contact ellenore@openheartsbigdreams.org for more information.

Made in United States
Troutdale, OR
12/29/2024

27394586R00021